Story Tense- Learn Tenses through Stories

Nilam Pathak and Anshuman Sharma

Published by Aegis India PL, 2019.

Also by Nilam Pathak

Story Tense- Learn Tenses through Stories
New Year Resolution: An Opportunity for Transformation
Swift Meditation: Power to Everyone
Think in English- Right Approach to Fluent English

Also by Anshuman Sharma

Story Tense- Learn Tenses through Stories
New Year Resolution: An Opportunity for Transformation
Swift Meditation: Power to Everyone
Think in English- Right Approach to Fluent English

Table of Contents

Copyright

Introduction

ENGLISH IS AN INTERNATIONAL language and it is required not only for global citizens, but also to do business around the world. In many countries, proficiency in English is necessary to grow in the career. As communication technologies and the connection between different communities and languages are improving, the importance of English language has increased. In countries like India, with different beliefs and spoken languages, English is the preferred language of communication between geographical regions. English has been the chosen language to share knowledge around the world.

Tenses in English have been the area of confusion for non-native speakers. Several methods are being employed by various educational institutions and governments to develop English language skills in their students and citizens. Methods include translation from native language to English and vice versa. Some people have tried to use digital technology to create new and innovative methods. Each methodology has its pros and cons. Some of these methods are effective, while others failed to deliver the required value.

We have tried to ease the process of learning tenses in English through this book.

This book discusses all the tenses of English in a unique way to hold the interest of the readers while enhancing their knowledge simultaneously. All the tenses in English are expressed with the story of two friends Tim and Jim, who works in an organization. The story starts with Simple Present Tense and continues through all the English tenses, to finish with Future Perfect Progressive. While covering a specific tense we have tried to deliver that specific part of the story in the same tense. The story uses most of the sentence types and structures for each tense, including affirmative, negative, and interrogative. It is required that the readers focus on the sentences used to express the story, rather than the story itself.

For each part of the story, move in the specified order of the book. For each tense read and reread the portion, till you become comfortable in creating your own sentences. Then move onto the next tense in order and repeat the process. It would be beneficial to revisit the book, whenever you feel the need to revise the tenses.

The more you read or listen to the story specified in different tenses, the better would be your proficiency in using tenses to express yourself. Remember that your focus is not the story, but the sentences with which the story is expressed. The purpose of the story is to provide a flow to the learning process.

Simple Present

IT STATES PRESENT FACTS. Simple present tense is used when an action is happening right now, or when it happens regularly (or constantly, which is why it is also called as present indefinite).

QUESTIONS TO BE ANSWERED

Generally, for Simple Present following questions are answered:

Who is he? Where is he? What does he do? How they do it?
Who are they? Where are they? What do they do? What do they eat?
Who is he? Where does he live? What does he do?
Who is he? What does he like? What does he dislike/ hate? Who helps him?
What is it? What does he want? Why does he want?

Action, event or state that happens in the present
Tim jogs every morning.
Usual, regular/ repeating action or habits
Tim never drinks cold water.
Tim doesn't jog every day.
Paris is in France.
I usually go shopping on weekends. I don't go to market on weekdays. Do you go to the park every morning?
Conditions (not actions) taking place at this moment.
They don't have any car.
He feels tired after a full day of work.

You are dumb.

General existence; stating a fact

Does earth go around the sun? The moon goes around the earth. The Sun doesn't go round the moon.

Dramatic narration (events)

Tim rides his bike, he kickstarts it, then he puts it into gear and drives.

Timetables

What time does the bus leave? The bus doesn't leave at eight. The bus leaves at nine.

EXAMPLES OF QUESTIONS

Are they happy?

Is she a nice girl?

Can you swim?

Do you have a dog?

Where are the children?

What is the time?

What can you draw?

How many stickers do you have?

Do the boys play football?

Do you like ice cream?

Do they like coffee?

Does she like hamburgers?

Does Carol play the guitar?

Does an elephant eat nuts?

Where do the boys play?

What do you like?

What do they like for breakfast?

What does she like?

Where does Carol live?

What does an elephant eat?

———◉———

Story – Simple Present

TIM IS A SOFTWARE ENGINEER. He lives in Bangalore. He works in a software company, which is one of the biggest organization in the world. His position in the company is "Team Leader". This is a responsible position in which he leads a team of seven junior software engineers.

Tim loves his job. He always works hard, just like his last six years in the company. The members of Tim's team have different designations. Coders with two years of experience are called Junior Software Engineer. People with two to four years of experience are known as Software Engineer. After four years of experience, good employees are eligible to lead a team. Tim is a good engineer and can lead a team well, therefore he is a Team Leader. After a couple of years, he can become an Assistant Project Manager. Tim reports to his Project Manager, who has twelve years of working experience.

The Project Manager of Tim likes him for his professionalism and sincerity towards his work. Tim always completes his work on time with his proper planning and management. He keeps a friendly environment within his team and is always ready to solve their problems. His team members respect and praise him for his knowledge and leadership. Tim is their role model. Tim's team members want to be like him in the future. They are learning new skills and technologies with every new project. Tim helps them and wants to develop a strong and efficient team.

Tim is a punctual man, who doesn't like people to get late for work. His team knows about it and everyone always reaches office before time. Tim thinks that people who are not punctual, cannot be sincere in their work.

He says "On rare occasions, if a person gets late that can be excused. But, if it becomes a habit, then strict measures must be taken."

Often, his colleagues ask him "What time do you think is right to leave the office, after a full day of work?"

Tim's reply is always the same "We should not try to display others our work and efforts, instead, we must put genuine efforts to get results. We need to complete the required tasks with our best endeavors within the allocated time, instead of waiting for the last day to finish. Once the task is complete in the right way, then we can always leave the office for home, even if it is before time."

People love his attitude towards work and life. He wants his team and everyone in his office should have a similar way of thinking.

Tim clearly understands the goals, which his company expects him to meet. Tim is also aware of the personal goals of each member of his team. He has worked hard to connect with his team members. He takes them to team parties often, so that they can connect with each other, personally. Tim knows that without the right connection within his team, it would be difficult for him to achieve work performance goals.

The office of Tim has a modern canteen with all up-to-date facilities and food items, suiting the taste of most of the people. Though the canteen does not serve meals, it is good for snacks and fast food. Tim always brings his lunch from home. Every morning, his mother cooks it for him. She wants Tim to eat fresh food to keep him healthy and active. It is tough for her to wake up early in the morning and prepare breakfast and lunch for her son, but she enjoys it.

Tim is a troubleshooter who is ready to solve any problem. His basic nature is to help others. His office mates come to him for honest opinions and to get solutions to their problems, both personal and professional. He never claims to be a guru, instead a friend who wants to reduce pain and give happiness to people.

Tim regularly takes interviews at his office for expanding his team. He wants good people to join his organization, to make it productive.

His interviews are simple, without complex technical questions. He wants to judge the attitude of the candidate, which is one of the most important characteristics of a person. Tim thinks that a person with the right attitude can be an asset for his team and his company, by adding substantial value through his competencies and skills. He knows that people with the right attitude are great learners and can get expertise in any area, in minimum amount of time. His most recent interview is as follows.

Tim: Do you go fishing on weekends?

Interviewee: I usually go to fishing on weekends, but I do not go to fishing on weekdays.

Tim: Do you always know the answer?

Interviewee: I always tried to put my best to give the answer, but I don't always know the answer.

Tim: Does your father ever put sugar in his tea?

Interviewee: He doesn't put sugar in his tea, but my mother never puts milk in her tea.

Tim: Does your father play guitar?

Interviewee: My brother plays the violin, but my father never plays guitar.

Tim: Do you go to the cinema on Saturdays?

Interviewee: We sometimes go to the cinema on weekends. We don't go to the cinema on weekdays.

Tim: Do you walk in the forest?

Interviewee: We don't walk in the forest woods. We never go to dangerous places.

Tim: How many legs does a caterpillar have?

Interviewee: An owl has two legs. A deer doesn't have two legs, instead, it has four. A caterpillar can have a different number of legs, depending on their size.

Tim: Is mercury solid at room temperature?

Interviewee: Water is liquid at room temperature. Silver isn't liquid at room temperature. Mercury is the only metal, which remains in the liquid state.

Tim: How to score points in basketball?

Interviewee: Pete takes the ball, he bounces it to the floor, then he throws and scores two points.

Tim: At what time does your bus leave?

Interviewee: My train leaves at half-past five, but my bus leaves after seven. We have enough time to talk.

Tim: When does your bus start?

Interviewee: My bus doesn't start before seven. My bus starts at half-past eight. I need some time for my dinner too.

Tim selected the candidate of this interview. The name of the candidate is Peter. He is smart. He instantly comes-up with the answer to the question asked, however complex. His answers are good and funny. Peter is now the part of Tim's team. Peter is a good addition to Tim's team. He is an organizational asset.

Simple Past

IT SPECIFIES THE ACTION, events or state that happened in the past or existed before now. It emphasizes that the action is complete or finished. It is sometimes called the preterite.

Example: Tim jogged yesterday morning.

QUESTIONS TO BE ANSWERED

Generally, for Simple Past following questions are answered:

Who were they? What did they do? Where did they go? What happened?
Who was she? What did she do? Whom did she meet? What happened?

Story- Simple Past

ONE EVENING, TIM WENT to a movie with his friend Jim. Tim and Jim worked in the same company. Jim met Tim when he joined the company three years back. One year back they both went to a movie at a multiplex. They saw a horror movie. This movie was a big-budget Hollywood blockbuster. The movie started at 6 PM. They both enjoyed the movie. Many people in the theater were terrified after watching the movie. Several viewers did not watch the full movie. They did not like the film. A minority of movie-lovers liked it so much that they wanted to experience it all again. Tim and Jim both liked the movie, but not as much to watch it again.

After enjoying the movie, both colleagues went to a restaurant to have dinner. The night was very beautiful, with the full moon shining brightly. They walked to the restaurant from the movie theater. The distance between both the places was about 500 meters. Both friends talked about their likes and dislike in movies. They were surprised to know that they had many common choices. Both liked action thrillers and horror movies. Even the choices of actors and directors were common. They decided to see many other movies together.

At the restaurant, they found that none of the tables was vacant. The manager of the restaurant told them that they should wait for 15 minutes, to get the table for two. They were lucky to get the table at the restaurant in just 10 minutes of wait. It was a nice ambiance inside the restaurant. Everybody was enjoying the soft music with their meals. Most of the people were either with their families or friends. Only one person was eating alone. He was sitting on a two-seater table, with one chair vacant. He was not looking around but was completely engaged in his eating. He was looking like a character from the movie, they just watched. Tim and Jim started to discuss the movie in which the antagonist was eating alone in a restaurant. It was fun to talk about the movie and comparing it with the man in the restaurant.

After 15 minutes the food was served. At the same time the single man finished his meal and went out of the restaurant. They were relieved to find that there was no incident similar to the movie, in which some dark forces had attacked the people in the restaurant. Tim and Jim thought that they are trying to see the resemblance of the movie in real life. They laughed loudly. People sitting at a nearby table looked at them and gave a smile.

The food in the restaurant was delicious. Both friends enjoyed it completely. Everything was in the right balance, which was giving a wonderful taste to every dish. The desserts were served to them after they finished their dinner. It was complimentary. Both were delighted to know about it. They appreciated the respect given to them and promised to visit the restaurant again. Just like the food and ambiance, the desserts were also enjoyable.

When Tim and Jim reached home their parents were awake. They were waiting for their sons to return after watching the movie. Their families were concerned about both the men, as they did not return to their home, after watching the movie. Instead of going straight to their house, they went to the restaurant for eating dinner, which was unplanned. They were late by more than an hour. They were wrong in not informing their families about their decision to eat dinner outside, which would make them late.

Both Tim and Jim accepted their mistake. They were apologetic about their actions. Both friends promised their families not to repeat the mistake again. They could understand the concerns of their parents who were unable to contact their sons. They should have informed their parents about their intention of going to a restaurant after watching the movie. It was a big lesson for both of them, which made them a better person.

At night Tim's mother came to talk to her son. She wanted to talk to him about the incident. She suggested him to forget about the incidence, but to remember the lesson. Tim listened to her with utmost attention. It was a great learning for him. Tim's mother asked a few questions to him.

Mother: Where did you meet Jim?

Tim: I met Jim at the office.

Mother: Did you have lunch with Jim yesterday?

Tim: I took lunch with Jack yesterday. I didn't have lunch with Jim yesterday.

Mother: Did Jim go to work on Saturday?

Tim: Jim didn't go to work on Saturday. Jim went to work on Friday.

Mother: Where did you go shopping last week?

Tim: I didn't go shopping last week. I did my shopping two days back.

Mother: Where did Jim travel last year?

Tim: Jim didn't travel anywhere last year. He traveled to London this year.

Tim understood that he should care for the people who care for him. He could feel the stress, which his parents must have felt, when they did not get any information about him. Tim's mother told him that mistakes are a way to learn in life, but we should never repeat them. Tim smiled and agreed. He was an improved person after the incident. He was happy to have a caring family. Tim's mother told him to sleep as she switched off the lights. Tim was very tired after a long day. He slept with a smile on his face to see good dreams.

That night Tim saw many good dreams. He never saw so many good dreams before, in a single night. He didn't want to wake up in the morning. He was enjoying his dreams. People forget dreams after waking up. He wanted to remember all his dreams. He decided to note all the dreams, which he remembered, in his journal. He wanted to tell about his dreams to his friends. It was a good way to entertain. Tim could remember only half of his dreams, but they were enough to engage his friends for twenty minutes. There were gaps in his dreams, which he decided to fill by himself. He was intelligent enough to know that a story of the dream should look complete. In fact, they all were sharing fictitious short stories with each other. Tim and his friends shared their dreams during their free time in the office. They all enjoyed sharing their dreams with each other. Many people in their office started to copy them by forming their own groups, to share their dreams of last night.

Simple Future

IT IS THE ACTION, EVENT, or state that will happen in the future.

QUESTIONS TO BE ANSWERED

Generally, for Simple Future following questions are answered:

Where will he go?
What will he do?
What will happen?
Who will come?
When will he start?

Action, event, or state that will happen in the future:
Examples:

Next month he will graduate from medical college.
How long will they be married by next week?
I hope you will not be disappointed?
I believe they will complete their work on time.

Promise or intentions:
Examples:

We will always help your family.
He will not give up.
I will reach the ceremony as soon as I can.
I won't tell anyone about it.

Story- Simple Future

NEXT MONDAY, TIM WILL be 29 years old. He will organize a birthday party at his office. He will give a birthday party to his friends. His birthday party will start after completing the office. Many people from his office will attend this party. The party will surely be fun. They will all enjoy the birthday party. Tim's friends will bring birthday presents and gifts for the birthday guy.

Tim's office will allow a small party in their meeting room, which will be attended by his department. Most of the people from his department will attend this party. It will be a good opportunity to connect with each other personally. The party will be over within half an hour. Tim's immediate boss will not attend the party, as he is going out of the town for official work. His General Manager will order soft drinks and snacks for the party. This will also be the right occasion for the General Manager of Tim's department to connect with his team. He will not miss the chance of talking to his department executives, personally. He will not discuss any official item with his team during the party. He would like to utilize the party to interact casually with his team members.

Tim's close friends have planned to surprise him on his birthday by organizing a dance party after office. They have ordered a big chocolate cake, which they will use to celebrate their friend's birthday. They know that Tim will be pleasantly surprised with a designer cake. He loves chocolate and they expect that Tim will appreciate the surprise. The cake will be full of ingredients, which would enhance the flavor of each bite of the cake. Everyone at the party will also love the taste of the cake. The organizers of the party have ensured that no one will know about the surprise, before its presentation. All invitees will see the cake only after it is brought from the bakery.

One of Tim's friend asked jokingly "Will you be 29 again, anytime in future?"

Tim replied with a smile "I will complete my 29th year on this birthday. Just the way I will not be 20 years old anytime in the future, I won't be 29 again. Nobody can be. If someone can do that magic, then everybody would like to learn the trick."

Jim was having a doubt. He asked, "When will the party start?"

He got the answer "The party won't start before 6 o'clock. I think it will be at 6:30 PM, only after everybody is out of the office."

One of Tim's junior asked, "Will boss attend the party?"

"No, he won't. He has a business meeting to attend, after office hours. He will go to Gandhi Place market to meet some clients."

Jim asked again "How will we reach the restaurant?"

One of Jim's associate replied "Some people will go alone. If you do not have any vehicle, you can join me in my car. Will you?"

Jim was happy to know that he will go to a restaurant with the help of one of his colleagues.

Tim wanted to dress well for his birthday party. He knew that it will be a special day for him and his team. They will all enjoy and have fun on his birthday party at the restaurent. Tim wanted to keep his birthday celebration minimal but enjoyable, and to make sure that everybody likes it. He will ask his friend Jim to help him shop for the clothes.

Tim thought "I will make sure that I look handsome on my birthday."

Jim will take Tim to the market to help him buy new clothes. Jim is an expert shopper, who will help his friend to get the best deal on new clothes and accessories. Jim will enjoy shopping for his friend. He will take some time-out of his usual schedule to go out with his friend Tim to guide him shop for his birthday items. As promised to their families, they will inform their parents about their shopping schedule.

They will go shopping on Saturday, which will be a weekly holiday for both of them. It will not be required to take any leave for going to market for shopping. They will go to the market in the afternoon, when the market will not be crowded. Jim will go to the three main shops, which he consider as best. He knows the choices of his friend and hopes that his selection of shops will be appreciated by Tim. They will go for lunch after shopping. Their families will not wait for them, as both men would have informed their parents, before leaving the market. They will return back to their homes before the evening. This time they will act more responsibly, based on their learning in the previous event when they reached home late. They will grow up to be sincere and mature men, who would care for their loved ones.

The birthday party is not going to affect the office work of Tim or his friends. They will complete their daily tasks and meet their responsibilities, without getting disturbed in any way. Tim will feel his importance rise for some time, due to his approaching birthday. Tim will behave elegantly as his birthday celebration date approaches near. Everyone will learn about giving respect to other people on their special day.

Tim's family is also planning a small family get-together on Tim's birthday. This will be a surprise for Tim on his birthday. They will not inform Tim about this gathering at their home on his birthday. They will plan well in advance to avoid conflict and overlap between different parties. They are aware that he will attend two other parties, first at his office and second at a restaurant with his friends. They will organize a family get-together only after he returns back from his second party with his friends. It means that the family get-together will start at night before dinner. Everybody will be excited about the family gathering and would be waiting eagerly for it. Birthdays and other family functions are the major events, when family members meet each other. Tim's parents will have to inform all nearby relatives to attend the get-together. Tim's parents will also arrange dinner for all guests. It will consist of the food items, which will suit the taste of all invitees. They will first prepare the menu for the dinner, which will then be ordered from a restaurant. Tim's family will ensure that everybody has a good time on their son's birthday.

Present Progressive

ACTIONS AND EVENTS happening in the present.

QUESTIONS TO BE ANSWERED

Generally, for Present Progressive following questions are answered:

Who is coming?
Where are they staying?
What are they doing?
What is he doing?
What is he thinking?
What are we planning to do with it?

Actions that are happening now (in the present moment):

Are you watching a movie?

I am not watching a movie, instead, I am watching my favorite show on TV.

Is your mother sleeping in the bedroom?

No, my father is sleeping in the bedroom. My mother is working in the kitchen.

Actions happening in the present, but not necessarily now (at this moment):

Tim is reading the book about Communication Skills.

Peter is studying hard for his competitive examination.

Usually, I reach on time, but this week I am getting late due to route diversion by police.

Definite arrangement (actions that will happen) in the near future:

Tim is meeting Jim in the afternoon.
Are they coming with us to the dinner tonight?
When is the meeting starting?

Annoying repeating actions:

You are always coming late.
You are always getting confused.
He is constantly trying to put him down.
This road is always overflowing with traffic.

Story- Present Progressive

TIM IS SITTING IN HIS room. It is morning time and Tim woke up a few minutes back. He is sitting, but still is half-asleep. He is feeling lethargic even after a full night sleep. He is waiting to get complete control of his body and mind, before starting the morning chores. He is looking out of the window. He is watching the Rose Garden located in the park. He is enjoying the view of fresh roses with different colors, which are looking beautiful. Right now, his mind is blank, as he is completely focused on the beautiful view of the Rose Garden. Every morning, he energizes himself for starting his day by looking at the roses in the garden. At this moment, he does not want anybody disturbing him. Tim feels like meditating, as it frees him from any thoughts, momentarily.

After some time, he started looking at other areas in the park. He could see the wind blowing, which is waving the leaves of the trees and plants slowly. Even the roses are moving slowly with the push of the wind, as if they are dancing on music. This music can only be heard by closing the eyes and focusing the attention on silence. Those flowers are looking like small and beautiful kids, who are meditating in the park. With every passing minute, Tim's mind and body are getting fresh. He is meditating in this experience.

There are many people present in the park. Some of them are walking or exercising. Many are sitting on the benches and enjoying the view of the park. A minority of people are not doing anything, maybe they are forcibly being sent to the park by their family to freshen up. They are trying to pass their time by lying on the grass, hoping to get a nap. People are walking at a different pace. Some are walking briskly, while others are walking slowly. Not only young people are walking fast, but we can find people of all ages trying to warm-up their bodies, through mild jogging.

People in the city are getting conscious about their health. A reasonable percentage of city dwellers are waking up early in the morning and taking out time for exercises, both physical and mental. People are becoming aware of the diseases they are getting, due to their present lifestyles. They are learning the right ways to keep themselves healthy. People who are not keeping their body fit and healthy can have a high probability of getting diseases.

Tim's mom asked, "When are you coming to the dining table for breakfast?"

Tim asked "What are you cooking? I am getting late for the office."

She replied back "I am not the reason that you are getting late for office. You wake up late and then keep sitting, looking outside the window, while wasting time."

Tim said "I am not wasting time, mom. I am meditating during that time."

"Whatever, I do not want you getting late for office."

After waiting for some time, Tim's mom asked again "Are you still sleeping?"

Tim replied hurriedly "Somebody else could be sleeping. I am not sleeping. I am not thinking about sleeping. There is no way you could find me sleeping."

Tim's mom smiled and teased him again "Are you watching television?"

"What are you saying, mom? Are you pulling my leg? I am not watching anything on TV. I am now getting up to get fresh."

She asked "Are you coming for breakfast? I am waiting for you."

He replied "I am not coming for breakfast immediately. Is anybody else coming? Are you serving breakfast to anyone?"

"I am not serving to anyone now. I am waiting for everyone to come down to the dining table. You all need to understand that I am also having tasks to complete. I am working hard to keep you all healthy. You all are disturbing my schedule."

Everybody in the house knows that the lady is losing her temper, which is not good for anyone. Tim's mom is just having fun while freeing her family from morning lethargy. Now, everybody is running around to be the first person to reach the dining table. Tim is hurrying to get into the bathroom for taking bath and getting fresh.

Half an hour later, everybody is sitting at the dining table, waiting for their breakfast. Mom is smiling. As always, her trick is working effectively. She is now getting ready to serve the breakfast on the dining table. Tim and his father are looking handsome. Both are wearing a formal dress with contrasting color tie. Tim is wearing black color shoes, while his father is wearing brown color shoes, which are matching their dresses. Both father and son are looking impressive. They are mentally getting ready for their offices and a long day of work. Tim's mother is also planning for her day's work. She is thinking about getting more productive in her tasks.

Tim asked his father "Are you traveling to Europe tomorrow?"

His father replied "I'm traveling to London tomorrow. I'm not traveling to Paris on this trip."

Tim's mother asked, "Where are we going to holiday this year?" Both, Tim and his mother started to look into the man's eyes with hope.

Tim's father replied "This time, we're not going to visit any new state in our country. But, we are going to Australia on holiday this year. Isn't it great?"

Tim jumped, shouting "You never stop surprising us. I'm sure that my day is going to be great today."

Tim asked his mother "Is uncle Joe taking his office team to dinner tonight?"

She replied "He isn't taking his friends to dinner tonight. This week, Joe is taking his family to dinner at a five-star hotel. He is changing himself and becoming a better family person."

Tim's father asked his son "What courses are your friends going to attend? What language are you studying?"

Tim thought for some time and replied "No, my friends are not showing interest in a language course. They are going to a business course. I am not studying Spanish. I am studying French and German. Everybody's thinking that I am planning to emigrate to Europe."

After breakfast, all three family members are now getting ready for their daily work. Tim and his father are going outside their home to their offices. Tim's mother is getting ready to complete several household tasks.

Past Progressive

THE PAST PROGRESSIVE (Continuous) is a form of the verb that shows the action or state was in progress (continued) in the past. It expresses the actions and events happening in the past.

QUESTIONS TO BE ANSWERED:

Generally, for Past Progressive following questions are answered:

Where was she staying?
What was she doing?
What was happening?
Where were they going?
What were they doing?

Actions and events that were in progress at a certain point in the past:

Yesterday afternoon we were speaking at a conference, so we could not come.
Were you studying all night long?
He was playing the whole afternoon.
Why was Raj acting strangely?
They were sleeping when the bell rang.

Annoying repeating actions in the past:

My teacher is always shouting.
He was always behaving strangely.

25

This man was behaving rudely.

Story- Past Progressive

YESTERDAY, TIM WAS working late in his office. He was working on a project whose deadline was approaching fast. Tim was working hard to solve a nagging problem. He was working with his team. Even his boss was staying late in the office. The client was demanding the completion of the project on time. The project was behind schedule because they were facing some critical problems in the development. They all were working very hard with complete sincerity. Everybody was putting their best to deal with the bottlenecks, which were slowing them down. Even after working long hours they were not able to resolve all the issues related to the project. Some of the team members were feeling frustration, but others were highly motivated. Tim was working at his peak performance level so that he could complete the task in a minimum amount of time. He was getting support from his team.

One of his team members was not feeling well. He was having a headache and was unable to work efficiently. Even after repeated suggestions from his team members, he was not going back to his house for resting. He was fulfilling his responsibility to work with his team for the successful completion of the project. Everybody in the team was having respect for this engineer, who was putting his job and responsibility above his own needs and body.

Most people in the team were getting repeated calls from their families, inquiring about the reasons for getting late.

Everybody was replying to phone calls, "I will be coming late today, as I am working on a very important assignment, which must be completed before today's midnight."

Tim's boss was observing the commitment shown by Tim and his team. He was happy to be working with a team of committed individuals. Everybody in his team was happy for getting the opportunity to work on an important project. The team was displaying professionalism and dedication towards their work. Everybody in the office was appreciating Tim for his leadership and management.

As Tim and his team were working on the project, his phone rang. The client was calling. Tim prepared himself for taking the call, assuming that the client representative was going to remind him about the deadline of the project.

The client asked, "Is your team working on the project, as per the requirements specified by us?"

Tim replied with confidence "Sir, my team was not working on anything other than specified requirements. We were working based on the exact document specifications, submitted by your company."

As Tim was waiting for them to raise any query, he could hear the caller on phone who was talking to his team on some important issue. There were some intense arguments, but Tim was unable to understand anything. Even though he was trying to comprehend the reasons for the dispute, but the voices were not clear. Even after waiting for four minutes, he was still holding the phone, hoping to hear the voice of the caller on his phone.

"Hello" Tim could hear a different voice, "Were you talking to anyone at eight from our company, last night? What were you doing when you got the call? Were you sending a mail to us about the developments of the project? Where were your team members working?"

Tim was surprised with the volley of questions, he replied "I wasn't talking to anyone at eight last night. Our team was busy working on your project." Tim asked the person on phone, "You were asking so many unrelated questions. What were you expecting?"

After a pause, the man said "We were thinking about changing some requirements of the project? We know that you all were working on the project based on our previous requirements and now we are giving you something new. Our top management was in the process of changing many systems in our company. Last week, our senior management was insisting on changing the requirements of the project. We were thinking about it. I was given the responsibility of talking to you about it. Nobody was interested in taking this responsibility."

Everything was getting complex and mysterious.

Tim was in the state of shock as he was listening to the words of the man on the phone. Everything they were working was getting junked by one phone call. His team was working so hard with sincerity, but now every requirement (on which they were working), was being modified.

He said "Sir, after several months of hard work we are on the verge of completing the project. We were putting our best resources for you. During the project contract sign-up, we were discussing a hypothetical situation like the present one. This project is complete, anything new will be considered as a new project."

As Tim was instructing his team to stop the work, everybody was shocked. Some team members were getting demoralized. Tim was explaining to them the reasons for the changes. He was explaining to them that the present project would be considered as complete and now they will be working on a new project. Their company was getting paid in full for the project they have completed.

Everyone in the Tim's team was happy as their project was getting completed. They were thinking about taking a break for a couple of days, before starting the project with new requirements of the client. The whole team was getting paid leaves for three days so that they could enjoy and unwind. Everybody was looking relaxed. They were the reason for saving the company from an expected big loss.

Everyone from the team was preparing the plans to go out with friends or family, before starting the new project. It was like recharging their bodies and mind, before starting working again with full force. Tim was happy and thankful to his team for working hard with dedication. He was also planning to go out with his parents to a nearby hill station.

He was thinking about having a complete break from his work and giving his full attention and time to his family.

Each one from the team was eagerly waiting for the day to get over. They all were starting to get in the mood of vacation. Some of the people from the team were already calling the agents and hotels for booking. They all were careful about not going to the same place as none of them wanted to meet each other during vacation. They all were working for long hours for several months together, now they wanted a break from each other too.

Everybody was happy and satisfied with the work they have done and were ready to take on the next challenge.

Future Progressive

IT IS A FORM OF THE verb that shows the action or state that will be in progress at some time in the future. It expresses actions and events happening in the future.

QUESTIONS TO BE ANSWERED

Generally, for Future Progressive following questions are answered:

Who will they be meeting?
What will they be doing?
What will be happening?
Where will it be going?
When will you be joining?

Story- Future Progressive

THIS WEEKEND TIM WILL be visiting the book fair at the exhibition center. Tim's friend, Jim will be accompanying him to the exhibition. Both will be enjoying their weekend together. It will be a nice time browsing books on different subjects. Tim will be looking for some specific books, which he is trying to find for the last year. He will be taking help from the staff of the exhibition to check for the location of those books. He would specify the names of those books on a paper form and would be submitting it to the main counter of the exhibition. They will be taking some time to search for those books in their database. If they find any of those books, then they will be informing Tim about it. If books are not available, then Tim won't be insisting on searching again. The exhibition executive will also be guiding them towards the location of those books. It will be exciting for Tim if he finds the desired books at the exhibition.

Jim will be helping his friend Tim to search for his books. After that Jim will be exploring books kept in the nonfiction section of the exhibition. Jim will be glancing all the new arrivals and would be checking the books of his favorite authors. He is also expecting to discover some good new authors. He will be showing more interest in the books related to self-improvement. He will also be meeting some of the authors who would be present at the exhibition. It will be a great learning experience interacting with the authors and understanding their views. Jim will also be meeting several other book readers. They would be discussing several topics in common interest areas.

Jim and Tim will also be attending a conference at the exhibition. Several prominent authors will be speaking at the conference. They will be sharing the summaries of their upcoming books, which will be appreciated by many listeners. This will also be a marketing opportunity for these authors to publicize their work. Everybody will be getting a lot of value at this exhibition.

The exhibition management will also set up several sitting areas, where book readers will sit and read the initial pages of their favorite books. They will also be setting up four cafés at each corner of the exhibition, which will be rectangular in shape. Visitors to the exhibition will consume the preparations of these cafés, which will be serving fast food and drinks. Each of these cafés will be allowing the readers to sit in their cafés and read books while sipping coffee and eating snacks.

People will be asking several strange questions about the exhibition management, days before the exhibition.

Questions: Will my family be having fun at your exhibition?

Answer: People not interested in books won't be having fun at the exhibition. If your family members love books, then they will surely be enjoying at the exhibition.

Questions: What will be the best mode of transport and path to follow for reaching the exhibition?

Answer: Any mode of transport will be fine for coming to our exhibition. We will be welcoming you as our guest. But, we won't be allowing any helicopter to land on the roof of the exhibition center.

(Everybody will be laughing after the answer.)

Question: What will you be doing at ten on the day of the Exhibition?

Answer: I won't be having dinner at that time as we will be busy preparing for the next day of books exhibition. We will be allowing you to serve us dinner if you want.

Question: When will I be reading the books, which I am going to buy in the exhibition?

Answer: You won't be reading them in the next 15 hours of buying books. We think that you will start reading those books only after a day of buying.

There will be many others at the exhibition who will not be enjoying the book fair. It is possible that they will not be finding the books of their interest. As the exhibition will be big with a large number of sections, many people will get tired even before covering the whole exhibition area. Kids and older people will be the first ones to get tired in the exhibition. Exhibition management will be arranging enough seats for tired people to rest. visitors who will not be finding the books of their interest would be leaving the exhibition early.

Many people who are online shoppers will also be visiting this exhibition. It will always be a great experience to feel new physical books while speaking to their authors. These people will be experiencing a new environment, which they would be loving.

For many people, it will be a fun outing with their families and friends. It will be more like a picnic, as they will be eating out and spending their time with books. People will be planning with their family members and friends to visit the exhibition. Everyone would be enjoying their nice get-together at the book fair. They will be buying books on several topics for reading and some books for gifting.

The exhibitors will not be allowing any carry bag inside the exhibition area. Many shop-lifters will be trying to steal costly books. In addition to a few restrictions, exhibition security would be keeping the eye on the visitors, with the help of cameras and security personnel. Some of the security personnel will be wearing civilian dresses, so that nobody recognizes them. They will be trying their best to identify the mischief-makers among the serious book lovers.

The exhibitors will be working hard to facilitate the visitors by helping them to browse the books and buy them. People will be allowed to pay for books in various ways, including cash, credit cards, online payments, and even mobile payments. Some salespeople will be standing near the payment counters to persuade the buyers to buy more. They will be presenting several new schemes on electronic products like e-books, video tutorials, and audiobooks. Some people will be finding it interesting and informative, while few shoppers will be getting irritated by the bothering sales-talk. The salespeople will be extra careful while dealing with disinterested people, showing no interest in buying their products. They will be persuading them, but up to a limit. Their manager will be supervising them for behaving decently with the buyers, at the payment counters. All the staff members of the exhibition will be caring for the visitors and buyers so that they leave the exhibition completely satisfied with the experience. The exhibition management will be trying their best to make the book exhibition a success.

Tim and Jim will be spending around two hours at the exhibition, before leaving for a nearby restaurant to eat their lunch. They will not be having any difficulty in choosing the dishes for eating, as their choices are not very different. They will be spending around an hour at the restaurant. They will be informing their families about their whereabouts, occasionally. They will be using phone calls and instant messengers to connect with their families. Their parents will be happy with the right actions taken by their sons.

Tim and Jim will be reaching home before time so that their parents do not get stressed. They will be arranging their new books in their bookshelves, nicely. They will start reading their first book just after dinner.

Present Perfect

THE PRESENT PERFECT is a form of the verb that shows the action or state was complete before the present. It expresses something that has just happened.

The Present Perfect is used to express:

Actions of duration that occurred in the past (before now) of unspecified time,

Actions that started in the past but continue to the present,

Actions that started in the past but stopped recently.

QUESTIONS TO BE ANSWERED

Generally, for Present Perfect following questions are answered:

What has she done?
What has happened?
What have they done?
How long has it taken?
Has the work finished?

Story- Present Perfect

TIM HAS JUST WALKED outside his office. He looked back, as someone has called him from behind. It was Nancy. She asked, "Have you finished the letter?"

Tim replied "I have finished the letter, but Jim hasn't finished the letter. He has completed it yesterday, but was rejected by the boss."

Nancy asked, "How long has he worked on it?"

Tim replied "I think he has worked on it for two hours. He hasn't worked on it for the whole day."

She looked relieved "Somebody told me that Jim wasted the whole day on the letter, but he hasn't. I think he must have completed it by now."

Tim agreed "He has always worked hard on his projects."

Nancy asked "Has Jim gone back to his home? I know that his roommates have not left the building."

Tim replied, "Maybe, he has some important work, therefore he must have gone."

Nancy said "How long has Arnold been your boss? I don't think he has been a good boss ever. He has already been tagged as the worst manager."

Tim smiled "Our boss hasn't worked here for long. He has been hired on a temporary basis. I think he has been asked to leave the job. It looks that he hasn't driven his car for the last two weeks. I know he has loved driving his car always."

Nancy questioned "Has Arnold ever completed his project the way client wanted? I don't think he has achieved any results before. It is possible that he has taken the help of other people to reach his present position."

Tim wanted to change the topic "Our boss has been in our head for long, let's forget him. Have you been on holiday this year? I haven't been able to go anywhere outside for last one year."

Nancy replied in excitement, "Yes, I have gone to the nearby hill station for two days. I have always enjoyed meeting new people. How many times have your relatives visited you this vacation? My relatives have visited us four times this summer."

Tim said "My relatives haven't visited us this summer. My parents have planned to go to one of our relative's place. We have already packed our bags, with all types of clothes. We have waited for this moment for a long time. I have bought new clothes and accessories for trekking. I have gone to the sports shop, which is located in the main market. They have sold many such gears in the last 10 days. They haven't been able to sell anything in the football section."

After Nancy has left for her home, Tim has taken out his phone to call Jim, his friend. Jim replied that he has completed his work before time and has left for home early. On the way, he has stopped his vehicle near the bookshop and has bought the latest mystery novel. He has always loved reading thrilling stories. Jim has pre-booked this novel a week back by submitting the booking fees at the bookshop. He has planned to finish it in the next three days. He has not been able to finish any novel in the last two years. This time he has decided to complete reading his new book in the next few days. He has promised himself to finish any book he buys in the future.

As Tim reached his home he asked his mom "Has the mechanic repaired the computer yet?"

His mom replied "He has already repaired the printer. He hasn't repaired the computer yet. He has consulted his senior about it."

Tim asked, "Has our neighbor parked their car at the wrong place again?"

She replied "Yesterday, they have parked in the wrong place. I think that today they haven't parked at the same place. They have learned their lesson."

Before leaving for his room he asked: "Have you cleaned my room?"

His mom smiled and said, "Yes, I have already cleaned your room, though I haven't cleaned our living room fully."

She asked Tim "Have you gone to books exhibition with Jim? Have you seen anyone from our locality at the exhibition?"

He said "Yes, I have gone with Jim. He has different taste in books. He had bought fiction books. I have not seen any acquaintance there, maybe they have gone to the books exhibition in a different time slot."

Tim has brought the books in his bag. Tim has learned a lot from books. They have been his best friend. He has created a big library in his room, which has been appreciated by all. He has created a nice setup in his room. He has kept a nice study table with a comfortable chair, at the corner of his room. He has installed the wireless Internet in his room, with a range covering his whole house. He has given the wi-fi password of the Internet connection to his parents for experiencing high speed data transfer on their devices. His room has been unique in the house with colorful curtains and lively design on the walls. He has painted some of the designs himself. He has bought the paint from a branded store, which also guided him with the techniques to paint the wall. He has become an expert in painting the walls. His mother has asked him to paint a nice design on the living room walls. He has not painted the walls yet.

He has a big project to complete in the office, which has engaged him fully. For the last few weeks, he has brought back work from the office to his home. For a few days, he has worked late into the night. He has worked hard for this project. He has taken the help from several people while working on problems. Everyone in the company has helped him. He has also been a good person, who supports other people in his company. On several occasions, he has guided his juniors to perform better. Everyone in Tim's team has learned about respecting and caring for others.

Past Perfect

IT EXPRESSES ACTION or state that was complete before some time in the past.

The past perfect is used to express:

-Completed action before another begins (both in occurred in thepast)

Example: After we had purchased tickets, we were able to enter the venue.

-Actions of duration before something happened in the past

Example: I had attended the all sports event for years without ever having to purchase tickets.

- Statements with conditions (in the past)

Example: If we had purchased tickets in time, we would have been able to enter the venue.

-Reported speech

Example: The official asked if we had purchased tickets.

-To show dissatisfaction with the past

Example: We wished we had purchased tickets on time.

QUESTIONS TO BE ANSWERED

Generally, for Past Perfect following questions are answered:

What had they done?
Where had I gone?
What had I done?
What had I seen?
Who had owned it?

What had they done?

⬥

Story- Past Perfect

LAST MONTH, TIM HAD gone to his relative's house with his parents. They had taken a taxi to go to the railway station. At the station, they had waited for one hour for the long-distance train. For waiting, they had chosen the place on the platform where the entry door of their allocated train compartment arrived. Most of the people were holding their luggage, they hadn't kept it down. Many passengers had hired the platform support staff and paid them for arranging their luggage.

Tim and his parents had also taken the help of two support people for getting their luggage safely on the train. They had paid half the agreed payment, even before they carried their luggage. As the train reached the platform, everybody had rushed towards it.

In the next 20 minutes, all passengers had adjusted their luggage, without much problem. Most of the people had found their seats. Some people were happy to find that they had got a window seat. Some people hadn't got the seats of their choice. They had requested the window seats while booking the tickets, but it was not accepted. These people had felt disappointment.

Tim asked his mother "Had I met uncle John and his family anytime in the past?"

His mother replied, "You had already met your uncle John when you were five years old, but you hadn't met his family yet."

Tim asked, "How many letters had you written to uncle John before?"

Tim's father said he hadn't written any letter before, though he had received several letters from many people. He hadn't felt motivated enough for writing back to anyone. He told that Tim's uncle John had complained about it several times, but he hadn't convinced himself yet to write.

Tim asked, "Where had they lived before they moved to Mumbai?"

Tim's mother explained "They had lived in Pune before they moved to Mumbai, but they hadn't been to Mumbai before. They had always loved Pune, which is a quieter and smaller place. Mumbai is far bigger and they had their own doubts about adjusting to its lifestyle. For the last several years, they are saying that they had started to like Mumbai. Initially, they had felt repulsion in humid weather. The humidity in the air had given them several skin problems. Now they had completely adjusted to it, both mentally and physically."

Tim's father asked his wife "Have you locked the door before we left?"

His mother smiled and said "I hadn't locked the door before we left. In fact, you had locked all the doors. I had checked them before we left for the railway station, so there is no need for concern." Tim had seen his father stressed, several times in the past. He had behaved similarly on several occasions before. He had started to forget things, maybe due to age. Tim had suggested his father several times that he should visit a doctor. But, he had always ignored it. Last week, Tim had requested his mother to force his father for consulting a doctor about his condition.

Finally, Tim's father had agreed to see a general physician, who was his friend. He hadn't gone to any doctor whom he didn't know. He had never been comfortable discussing his medical records with any new doctor. He had many friends who were professional doctors. He always had a problem with trusting new people. He had always taken a lot of time, in fact a few years, to build trust with people. Maybe, it is because he had many bad experiences in his past.

Tim's father had started his business when he was only 22 years old. He had not taken any help from anybody, including his own family. He had created his innovative product at a minimal cost. He had used the savings from his pocket money to develop the product. Luckily, he had received a lot of attention after many people saw and experienced the product. Numerous buyers had even paid him in advance to develop the customized product. He had even received investment from a few high net worth individuals. He had proven his competencies to the world. He had never taken any help from anybody. According to him, the investors had given him money, only because they trusted him to multiply their investment. During those days, Tim's father had become a magician, who had the ability to multiply money.

Tim's father had requested on several occasions to his son to join his business, but every time Tim refused. He also had the same thinking pattern as his father. He had decided to build his own company. Therefore, he had joined a software company to learn the tricks of the business. For the last several years, he had involved himself in several areas of his company. He had also made sure to learn about new domains, which would help him to make his future business successful. His father had always appreciated his efforts. He had even proposed to invest in his son's company, but Tim had not shown any enthusiasm for the idea. He had tried his best to connect with other investors, who could invest in his business. He had got success in some areas, but also experienced failure in several others.

Tim had always enjoyed the train journey with his parents. The train journey had given them the opportunity to sit with each other for several captive hours. They knew about enjoying the train journey because they had travelled by train several times in the past. They had rarely experienced such a beautiful time together. In the train, they had all the time for each other, as they had disconnected themselves from their work and social life. Tim's mother had never been on a long-distance train before her marriage. She had experienced the fun of long-distance travel only after Tim was born. She was afraid of a long train journey because she had not experienced it before. She had heard about the problems on long journeys. She had tried her best to avoid the train journey citing various excuses, but could not avoid it due to the insistence of Tim's father. After the journey was over, she had become an advocate of a long-distance train journey. She had enjoyed it fully.

Since that day, this family had never missed any chance to travel by train.

Future Perfect

IT EXPRESSES THE ACTION, event or state that will be complete before some time in the future.

The future perfect is used to express:

-Actions that will start, and will be completed at some point in the future

Example: When he leaves, they will have finished the movie.

-Actions that occur in the future and will continue beyond a certain point in the future

Example: This summer, I will have been playing volleyball for four years.

QUESTIONS TO BE ANSWERED

Generally, for Future Perfect following questions are answered:

What will he have done?
What will have happened?
What will they have done?

Story- Future Perfect

NEXT MONTH, TIM WILL have worked in his company for seven years. Everybody will like to celebrate this occasion and congratulate Tim. Before that day, Tim and his team will have completed their project, on which they have been working for one year. Though they will not be getting any problem with their project, Tim will have prepared his team for it. They will have planned well in advance about dealing with any problem related to their project. That experience would have made them smarter and competent.

Tim's manager asked him "Will you have completed the project before the end of the month?"

Tim confidently replied "We will definitely have completed the work before the end of the month. I expect that my team will have given you the final presentation before the deadline. But, we won't have included any new requirements, which we will get."

Manager asked, "Will the two members of your team, who were on leave, have arrived before the final submission?"

"One of them will have returned back before the presentation. Another person who lives in another state won't have arrived before the final submission. He will feel sorry to have missed the fun we will have after completion and submission of the project. I hope that they will have enjoyed their vacation and join back fresh, ready for the next challenge."

Manager asked, "How many leaves will you have taken, before the final submission?"

Tim replied "I will have taken only one leave before the completion of this project. My team won't have taken more than six leaves in total, before the final submission."

"That is impressive. If everything goes according to plan, then I will have recommended your team for reward, so that they feel recognized and motivated."

Tim was happy "My team will surely appreciate it. The reward will motivate them to work harder for the next project. They will have gotten ready for long working hours by the time the next project starts."

The manager agreed "I am sure that by the time you complete this project, I will have recommended the reward for your team, which they truly deserve. This reward and appreciation will motivate several other employees to have work harder in our company."

In September, Tim will have lived in his house for fourteen years with his parents. Before the fifteenth year starts, Tim and his family will have captured several memories in the house. They will have the urge to renovate their home. Before that day, Tim's parents will have struggled to take out substantial money for a house renovation, as they would want to save for their son's future. Tim will have been trying to convince them for several months to invest money in the house. Even though he will have seen the problems associated with diverting the money from savings, he will have understood its importance.

Before the renovation of the house begins, Tim will have completed his present project in the office. He won't have faced any difficulty in completing it. In fact, he and his team will have enjoyed the experience. Just before the final submission, they will have worked together on the project for more than 2000 hours. They would have understood each other well, including their likes and dislikes. Some of the team members will have met each other's families.

The renovation of the house will be awarded to a contractor by Tim's father. He will have known the contractor for some time and must have appreciated his work before. The contractor would have quoted a reasonable estimate for completing the work. He will have promised to complete the work on time. Tim's family won't have given the full amount in advance, instead, they will pay only the partial amount. They will have decided the payment schedule based on the work completed. The contractor would have calculated the total cost and added his margin to it, for quoting the price of the work. He will have quoted a reasonable price, which will be acceptable to Tim's father. He will have appreciated the honesty of the contractor for rational quotation, without hidden costs. It is important that the contractor will have given the quality of the work as per the expectations of the family, to retain respect and appreciation.

In the month of September Jim will have been out of his college for five years. He will have completed five years of work experience. The present company will have been his second company. He will have worked for two years in his first company, while three years in the present company. He will have had many friends in his first company, who will still be connected with him on social networks. By the time he will complete five years of experience, he will have worked on four projects overall. Jim's work experience will have helped him to get the calls from other companies for the job. He will have analyzed all the job offers based on work profile and monthly earnings. He will have even consulted his friend Tim for suggestions. As always, Tim would have told him about looking for job satisfaction, instead of earnings.

Tim will have said "It is important that you enjoy your job, instead of just looking for your monthly payment. If you like your job, you will perform well in it. Performance leads to higher earnings."

Jim will have thought about the time he and Tim enjoyed together while eating, watching movies and attending books exhibitions. He would have felt the strong urge to continue his present schedule. He will have decided to remain in the present company and keep his friends.

Tim would have appreciated the decision of Jim about staying with the company. Tim will have missed his friend. Tim will have been delighted to hear the decision of Jim. This event will surely have made them even better friends. Tim will have recommended his manager about improving the monthly earnings of Jim so that everyone benefits.

Both friends will have known that they cannot be together in the coming years, as their career will take them on different paths. In the next few years, they will have to change their companies, cities or even countries. They will have to keep in touch with social networks, messages, and calls. In the future, their friendship will have grown into a family friendship, with both families regularly connecting with each other.

Present Perfect Progressive

IT EXPRESSES THE ACTION or event that started in the past and continued until the present.

-This means that the action itself began in the past. However, it continues to the present and has not yet stopped. It is still occurring as the sentence is written or read.

Example: Peter has been eating for hours.

-It can also refer to actions that started in the past but just recently stopped.

Example: Pete has been studying all day and now he is ready for the examination.

-Additionally, this tense can refer to something that is a relatively new habit that has been happening for some time. In this sense, it takes on the general meaning, "lately" or "recently."

Example: Recently, I have been eating a lot.

He has been jogging lately.

QUESTIONS TO BE ANSWERED

Generally, for Present Perfect Progressive following questions are answered:

What have they been doing?
Where have they been going?
What have they been doing?
What has he been doing?
What have they been thinking?

Story- Present Perfect Progressive

TIM AND JIM ARE GOOD friends who work in the same company. They have been eating together on weekends since Jim joined the company three years back. When Jim became part of the company, Tim was his Team Leader. Both became good friends, since that time they have been enjoying time together. They have similar taste and hobbies, therefore, they have been going out together to watching movies and eating food. They have been helping each other in office by supporting and solving each other's problems.

Tim's mother asked, "What have you been doing lately?"

Tim replied, "I have been missing my exercises lately. I haven't been going to the gym due to work."

Tim's mother asked, "How long have you been working on the project?"

Tim said, "We have been working on the present project for around a year. Most of the people in my team haven't been focusing on their personal life for the last few months. We all have been working to finish the project by next month. Our customer has been making changes in the project consistently, disturbing our plan. My team has been eagerly waiting to work on a new project, we all are now bored by its delay."

Tim's mother agreed, "Work has been getting less interesting due to the automation of most of the tasks. I do not know much about IT (Information Technology), but I know many good companies have been able to make work interesting. Maybe, your company hasn't been able to understand the importance of planning till now. As business is shaped by market and competition, I am sure that they have been thinking about it, though not as a priority. Have you been updating your manager on it lately?"

Tim replied in affirmative "Yes, I have been talking to him about the business issues regularly. Somehow, he hasn't been showing interest in it. Maybe, he has been busy in something."

Tim often travels to New York for project work. He has been meeting the client in the city for the last one year. They have been discussing the development and changes to be made in the project. For the last few weeks, they haven't been meeting face to face, instead, they have been communicating on phone and through e-mails. Digital communication has been an effective way of sharing information. People have been using it for their personal and professional communication. Governments haven't been preventing the leakage of information through the Internet. Technology has always been both boon and menace for humanity. People have been using technology to improve their lives and productivity. Technology has also been instrumental in the developing deadly weapons, which has killed scores of people.

Tim has been enjoying his trips to New York. He has been staying at the same hotel, which is located near the client's office. Due to his friendly nature, he has been successful in making the main official in the client's company as his friend. After every business meeting, they have been going out to enjoy a coffee at Starbucks.

At each business trip, Tim has been busy since morning till evening. He hasn't been meeting his college friends and few relatives living in New York. Several of his friends have been requesting him for a get-together, but he hasn't been able to spare time from work. He has been planning to get some personal time but every time something crops up, engaging him in work. Though he has been calling them and regularly sharing his details on social networks, he hasn't been able to meet any of his personal contacts.

His mother has been suggesting him to keep the proper balance in professional and personal life. He has been reading about it online and in books. He knows that if he hasn't been managing time, then it will cost him his peace of mind. He has been ignoring his personal contacts and hobbies for the last few years. Jim is the only person who has been accompanying him for several years in non-official tasks. They have been enjoying each other's company to unwind.

Tim's father has been insisting that he should expand his friend's circle. He has not been using his weekends to relax and enjoy. He has been completely engaging himself in his work.

Tim keeps telling "I have been enjoying being in stress and dealing with deadlines. I have been telling this to my family and friends. They haven't been supportive in understanding my philosophy. Personal and professional life have been overlapping for me, as I enjoy working and it is my hobby." People in the company are surprised to find that Tim has been keeping his high level of energy, even after long working hours. It is possible that he has been perceiving his work differently. He has been loving his work since his first day in the company, and still loves it.

Tim's experience has been challenging since the beginning of his career. He has been instrumental in taking many initiatives, which has enhanced the profitability of his company. The senior management of the company has been appreciating Tim for his efforts. Though there hasn't been a substantial increase in his pay, his job profile has been getting better, with every passing year. As a Team Leader, he has been taking the responsibilities to go to the business meetings with clients. Tim has been visiting several cities, including New York.

Due to accepting more responsibilities, he hasn't been taking care of his health. Tim's weight has been increasing since he joined the company. He has been overweight for two years now. His family has been concerned about it, but Tim is not ready to compromise on work. Tim's mother tried to convince her son "We all are watching you work hard. You know that we have been very supportive of your choices. We haven't stopped you from doing anything. We know that your work is an important part of your life, but your health has been deteriorating since the day you started working. This cannot continue forever. Previously, you have been taking care of your health, but now I see carelessness. What has happened to you?"

Tim was able to understand the concern of his mother. He has been trying to balance his work with personal life.

Past Perfect Progressive

IT EXPRESSES THE ACTION or event which started in the past and continued until some point in the past (up to another event in the past).

Example: It had been raining for two hours before flooing the roads.

The past perfect progressive is used to express:

-Duration of a past action (only up to a certain end point)

Example: The athelete had been working-out for an hour before she rested.

-Showing cause of an action

Example: Sam went bankrupt because he had been overspending.

QUESTIONS TO BE ANSWERED

Generally, for Past Perfect Progressive following questions are answered:

What had they been doing?
Where they had been doing?
What had she been doing?

Story- Past Perfect Progressive

JIM'S ELDER BROTHER is a businessman. He had been struggling for several years before his business finally took off. He had been a hardworking man in his job, which he got after finishing his graduation. He had been a good manager to his team, as he was emphatic to his team-mates and cared for them. He had been providing great service to the customers. Many times, he hadn't been sleeping well while on tours. He had always been dedicating himself fully to his work. Strangely, he had been feeling energetic, while working hard. According to him, he had been learning in the process and becoming a better professional. People in his organization had been getting difficulty in understanding his philosophy, which did not seem to be usual. He had been setting examples for others to follow. People still had been missing him in his previous company.

During his job days, he had been working hard, without caring for his health. He gained weight because he had been eating pizza two times in a day. He had been an energetic person, who would take risky decisions with full confidence. He had always been taking full responsibility for his decisions, even if they were wrong. He had been suffering setbacks due to his quest to get results, but it also made him a good manager who gets results.

The other day, Tim asked Jim, "How long had your brother been working to create his business?"

Jim replied "He had been working for several years on it. Till now, he hadn't been getting the desired results."

Tim agreed "Building a business had always been difficult, taking a lot of time for entrepreneurs. People had been sacrificing constantly to develop their companies. It had never been easy. It always had been a risky proposition."

Jim said "I had been observing my brother slogging for long hours at his workplace. For the last couple of years, he had been getting results for his efforts. He had always been customer-centric, focused on their satisfaction with providing constant support 24x7. His clients had been loving him for his professionalism and troubleshooting skills. Till now he hadn't been able to get great success. But, he had been successful in keeping himself satisfied with the results of his company."

Many people doubt, "Had Jim's brother been enjoying his work?" Jim's brother has always been enthusiastic about the work he is doing. He hadn't been wasting his time in the work he did not enjoy. He had been clear about the direction of his life.

At several occasions, it had been confusing for him to make decisions with limited resources and budget. But, he had been able to take the right decisions for his business. His team had been supporting him in his decisions. He had been following through his decisions with strong actions. He had been hiring good people to support him in his work. It had been a great learning experience for the people working with him. He had been acting like a good manager and mentor for his team members. They all had been loving working with him, as it was always been an enriching experience for everyone in his company.

Jim had been thinking about joining his brother at work. He had been yearning to help his brother in his business. Jim knows that his brother had been indicating his desire to be in a business partnership with him. Jim had been failing to get the clarity in his mind about the direction to be taken. Jim had been thinking about asking his friend Tim for his suggestions.

Jim and Tim had been enjoying their time with the company for several years. They had been working and enjoying together. They had been caring for each other as good friends. Tim had been ignoring several good jobs offers only to be with his friend Jim. He had been sacrificing a lot for his friend Jim. Jim had been hearing about it through other people. Both of them had been knowing that they cannot stay in the same company for long, as they have their own career direction. Both had been trying to extend this separation as much as possible. They had been enjoying their fun time together. They had been going out for movies, exhibitions, and food, as their choices are similar.

Jim hadn't been getting the clarity about his next course of action. He loves his brother and had been thinking to help him by joining him. He had not been able to convince himself leaving his friend Tim behind and start fresh with new friends. Jim had been discussing his confusion with his brother and also with Tim. Both well-wishers had been suggesting him to think freely and take the direction with which he feels comfortable. Even though Tim and Jim's brother had been desiring to have Jim's decision in their favor, but they want happiness for Jim. They know that if they force Jim for a favorable decision, then they hadn't been behaving honestly. They had been clear about allowing Jim to take his own decision.

Jim had been giving indications to his brother about his interest in continuing with his present job so that he could learn and also spend some more time with Tim.

Jim had been saying to his brother "Finally, I would have to be in your company, but for now I had been feeling like putting a couple of years more in my present company."

Jim's brother smiled and said "I had been knowing about it for some time. It is fine with me, but after two years you must come and join my company as a partner."

Jim agreed "You had always been a great brother. I had always been honest in following my promises. I will join you after the agreed time."

Tim had been waiting for Jim's decision for a long time. He had been expecting Jim's decision in his favor. Since that day, they had been making plans for their weekend fun. They had been visiting new restaurants, multiplexes and books exhibitions and many other places of fun.

Future Perfect Progressive

IT EXPRESSES THE CONTINUOUS action that will be completed at some point in the future. The future perfect progressive tense is used to express actions that will start in the future (they have not yet started) and will only last for a set amount of time.

Example: Next spring, you will have been acting for two years.

The future perfect progressive is used to express:

-Actions that will have a specific timeframe in the future

Example: We will have been sleeping for two hours when the bell rings.

-The cause of something in the future:

Example: You will have a solid retirement fund as you will have been saving for thirty years.

QUESTIONS TO BE ANSWERED

Generally, for Future Perfect Progressive following questions are answered:

What will they have been doing?
What will he have been doing?
What will they have been thinking?

Story- Future Perfect Progressive

TIM WILL BE ATTENDING a conference in Milan next week. He will be ready for it a day in advance as many people from his company will have been waiting to get their tickets from their Team Leader, Tim. All these people will have been waiting eagerly to attend the conference. Most of them will have been making plans for shopping and watching new places. They will have been collecting the required information about Milan from different sources.

Tim will also be a speaker at the conference. Even though he will have been working hard on his project, he will still be fresh for the trip to Milan. He will have been working on his presentation for several weeks before the presentation. He will have been meeting several of his seniors to get suggestions about the content of the presentation. He will make sure that his presentation at the conference is among the best.

Tim will have been getting good experience in his company before he gets a lucrative job offer from any other company. He will have been thinking hard and consulting his well-wishers before he decides to leave his job. In the new organization, he will have been adjusting to the environment, before he feels comfortable while working. He will have been working hard to connect with his team before he motivates them to enhance his team productivity. He will have been talking to his customers before they start to like him. Tim's team will have to trust him before they could have any connection with their new manager.

Tim's boss asked, "How long will you have been working on the present project?"

Tim replied "I'll have been working on the present project for two years by next month. I won't have been getting any problem in the project for the last year, making it one of the most productive years for my team."

Tim's boss was surprised "Two years have been a long time. You should not neglect your health, instead, you should keep a proper balance in everything. How long will you have been working with this company by the end of this financial year?"

Tim smiled and said "Are you thinking about giving me a raise? I will have been working here for seven years, by the end of this financial year. In fact, most people in my team will have been completing three years, by the end of this financial year. I'm sure that our human resource department would have been thinking about giving us all a 20% raise in our pay."

Tim's boss said "I do not know about it. How long will you have been talking about it with the human resource department?"

Tim replied with a sigh "We all will have been talking about it for at least two years, by the end of this month. I am sure that we have not been making any impact on their thinking, even with all our efforts. They have their rigid thinking pattern, which they will strictly follow."

Tim's boss tried to ignore the discussion and asked, "How long will Jim has been working with his present team?"

Tim replied "He will have been working with his present team for one and a half years, by the end of next quarter. Before that, he was working with me on my team. Therefore, he won't have been working with me for around two years, by the end of this financial year."

After a pause, Tim asked his boss "How long will your son have been studying in engineering college when he got his degree?"

Tim's boss replied with a little pride "He will have been studying in engineering college only for three years before he gets his degree by the end of May. He has been an intelligent student, who could clear his several semester examinations simultaneously."

Tim was impressed "He seems to be an intelligent person. I am sure he will have been in the senior management position in his job, even before he turns 30."

Tim will have been enjoying the casual conversations with his boss, for the next few years. He has been planning to stay in the company for a minimum of two years more. By the time he leaves his job in the present company, he will have been completing around a decade with the organization. His friends will have been trying to convince him to reverse his decision before he completes his notice period with the company.

Tim has been an asset to his present company, by completing complex tasks and projects. Tim will have been getting a lot of new job offers from different companies before he submits his resignation. He will have been fighting the urge of leaving his present company and to change the direction of his life. By the time he thinks about leaving his present job, Jim will have been out of the company for one year. Jim will have been thinking about leaving the present company, before joining as a partner with his brother. Initially, Tim will have been feeling bad about being alone in the company without Jim, but he will be changing his perception. He always knew that they cannot stay in the same company together, forever. He will have been training his mind for several years before Jim tells him about his decision of leaving the company. Tim will have been in the state of mild shock before he finally recovers and appreciates Jim's decision. They will have been good friends for several years before Jim leaves the company.

Tim and Jim always knew that they will have to follow a different career path, even if they are good friends. They would have been promising to each other to remain in constant touch, even after their direction and career goals change. They will have been working hard and taking challenges before they earn the senior management positions in their companies. They will be good bosses and great friends.

Tim and Jim have been good friends and they will always be great friends.

About Authors

NILAM PATHAK

Nilam is an International Published Author, Management Consultant & Specialized Corporate Trainer in Human Resource Management and Communication Skills. She has worked with leading international brands to support them in enhancing the performance of human resource. She is the director of 'Conversational Skills', a personality development institute, based in India.

ANSHUMAN SHARMA

Anshuman is an entrepreneur and investor and has been instrumental in nurturing many successful companies. He has created several profitable companies in various domains. He is also involved in supporting the development of several other organizations. In business, his interests lie in cutting-edge technologies and innovative services.

His guidance has helped many businessmen, investors, and entrepreneurs to succeed in their objectives. He has also supported several entrepreneurship cells and incubation centers.

About the Author

Nilam is an International Published Author, Management Consultant & Specialized Corporate Trainer in Human Resource Management and Communication Skills. She has worked with leading international brands to support them in enhancing the performance of human resource. She is the director of 'Conversational Skills', a personality development institute, based in India.